I SAID WHAT I SAID

AND THE UNIVERSE PROVIDED

Janice Jacobs

Janice Jacobs
I Said What I Said and the Universe Provided

Published by Spines
ISBN: 978-965-578-770-2

Dedication

Helen V. Perry

To my Guardian Angel for believing in me and loving me unconditionally.

Nakia Kristina LaBat

A sweet angel and tender spirit who rose above her physical pain to spread laughter and joy to everyone she encountered.

Chanze Jacobs

I thank the universe for bringing you into my life to be my daughter. I hope as soon as you find your inner light, you'll embrace it, trust it, and never tolerate fear. After all, you are more powerful than you know.

Orginell Chatman Harris

Thank you for giving me life. Mommy, I Love You!

Philippians 4:6-7

Do not be anxious about anything, but in everything by prayer and supplication with thanksgiving let your requests be made known to God. And the peace of God, which surpasses all understanding, will guard your hearts and your minds in Christ Jesus.

Contents

Job 22:28 — 9

Preface — 11
Janice Jacobs

1. STAY IN THE FLOW! — 15
Janice Jacobs

Albert Einstein — 19

2. THE UNIVERSE KNOWS THE WAY — 21
Shirley Ryan, PhD, CCHT

Isaiah 55:11 — 27

3. I WAS BORN FOR THIS! — 29
Jewel Diamond Taylor

Oprah Winfrey — 35

4. FOLLOW YOUR PASSION — 37
Rawlvan R. Bennett

Proverbs 3:5 — 45

5. WHEN GOD TELLS YOU TO MOVE... MOVE! — 47
Brenda Thompson

John Mitchell — 51

6. THE D-ATTITUDES, MY METHOD FOR
MANIFESTING — 53
Michael Brundy

Francis Bacon — 57

7. A TRULY 'OZ' MOMENT — 59
André Pittmon

Proverbs 16:9 — 63

8. MY UNSEEN CONVERSION — 65
Rev. Dr. Angelo V. Chatmon

Mark 11:24 — 69

9. BREATHE, BELIEVE AND RECEIVE — 71
Carla Sparks

Jeremiah 29:11 — 75

10. WHEN RAINSTORMS (AND TRAFFIC JAMS) OPEN
    DOORS   77
    Martin L. Howard II

    Romans 8:28   85
11. FULFILLING YOUR LIFE CALLING   87
    Lamont Harris

    Proverbs 3:6   91
12. OVER COMING INSECURITIES   93
    Marquetta DeVille

    Samuel 3:10   95
13. JUST STOP   97
    Lynnis Woods-Mullins CHHC, CLC, CPI

    Genesis 21:17   101
14. GOD HAS HEARD YOUR PRAYER   103
    Canise Lewis

    Matthew 21:22   107
15. MY (GOD'S) HOUSE   109
    Charmaine Singleton

    Isaiah 41:10   113
16. DETERMINED BEYOND MEASURE   115
    Shayla St Clair

    Luke 1:37   117
17. MY JOURNEY HAS JUST BEGUN   119
    Merry Adeleye

    Paulo Coelho   123
    Afterword   125
    Notes   127
    Notes   129
    Notes   130
    Notes   131

Job 22:28

"Thou shalt also decree a thing, and it shall be established unto thee: and the light shall shine upon thy ways."

JANICE JACOBS

Throughout my life, I have been fascinated by stories of individuals who were able to turn their dreams or desires into reality. It started during my childhood; I came across a story involving actress Natalie Wood. As a teenager wandering through the corridors of a prominent film studio, Natalie expressed her desire to marry the man featured on a movie poster to her mother. That man happened to be none other than Robert Wagner. She went on to marry him twice. Actor Jason Momoa has a similar story. Momoa has admitted to having a childhood crush on Lisa Bonet, whom he first saw on television at the age of eight. They eventually met in 2005 at a jazz club in New York City. The couple hit it off, and their relationship blossomed into romance. Momoa's childhood dream came true when he finally won the heart of the woman he had admired since childhood.

The account of Oprah Winfrey's path to securing the role of Sofia Johnson in Steven Spielberg's renowned 1985 film, "The

Color Purple", is widely known. As an avid reader and lover of the book, Oprah made a habit of carrying copies around to share with others. Despite having no prior acting experience and being unaware of the movie's production, she expressed her fervent desire to be a part of it. The Universe seemed to be listening, as she was invited to audition for a role without being informed of the actual title. Given her familiarity with the book's content, Oprah quickly realized the purpose of the audition. In her own words, she had never before wanted anything as much as that particular part. Despite not receiving immediate feedback, she firmly believed that she had been turned down for the role, leading her to attend a health spa for weight loss. While on the track, she was informed to stop and pick up a phone call, and asked to cease losing weight or she would jeopardize her chances of being cast. She states it was the happiest day of her life when she learned she had been selected for the part.

I remember watching Oprah's TV show and seeing Hollywood actor Jim Carrey who has also shared an inspiring tale of manifestation. Confident in his abilities, he manifested his success by writing himself a ten-million-dollar check. Remarkably, his manifestation transformed into reality when he landed the lead role in the 1994 film "Dumb and Dumber", allowing him to cash the same check years later.

Another story that never fails to make me smile is the birth of Vanessa Williams. Her parents proudly announced her arrival with the words, "Here she is Miss America". How amazing is that? It's like destiny was calling out to her even before she was born. Then there is Lady Gaga who during a 2011 interview, after her rise to fame, disclosed how she persevered in repeating a positive affirmation to herself repeatedly, convincing herself of her imminent celebrity status. I love these stories, and one thing they all had in common was the great energy behind their intention. They had hope, excitement, and anticipation. They have captured my interest as I have encountered numerous instances where events aligned effortlessly, or occurrences beyond the usual seemed to indicate a higher power was watching over me ordering my steps. It evoked in me an awareness of being carried along by a compelling force, or as I like to say, a state of being in synchronicity with the universe.

This book is filled with stories of both powerful and gentle experiences, as well as personal interpretations, understandings, and acceptances. While we each have our unique way of experiencing and interpreting God's revelations and presence; we all have a story worth sharing… That, I know for sure.

CHAPTER 1
Stay In The Flow!

JANICE JACOBS

I RECALL AN INCIDENT IN 2015, during a tough time when my younger sister Kimberly was facing her last days as she battled breast cancer, an emotional moment took place. It was me, my older sister and three of Kimberly's four children gathered around her bedside. In a heart-to-heart talk with Kimberly, we talked about how she wanted to be remembered. Kimberly was a huge lover of small animals, so she wanted people to connect her with them. Inspired by her passion for small dogs, we all wholeheartedly agreed. Remarkably, just a few days later, during my morning drive home following a late night spent with Kimberly, an advertisement for an estate sale caught my attention as I exited the free-way. Estate sales were a shared hobby between my daughter and myself, as we frequently made it a pastime activity on the week-ends. Typically, these sales would extend over several days, there-fore it was important to attend on the opening day.

Despite feeling somewhat tired from my drive from Vallejo back home to Sacramento, I decided to stop by the sale which was conveniently close to my home. Normally, I look throughout the house at all the items for sale. However, on this occasion, as I walked into the home, my attention was immediately drawn to a small figurine. I felt like it was waiting for me. I picked it up, and with amazement, I knew that it was indeed waiting for me. The figurine portrayed two small dogs and two small cats encircled in a paw-holding stance, aptly suited for commemorating Kimberly, and more remarkably, incorporating me and my other two sisters into the picture of solidarity. Four beings in perfect unison. I was not looking for this figurine, but the universe knew what I needed and assisted me in getting it. All I had to do was allow myself to flow in the spirit.

Another incident happened earlier in 2004. At the time I loved the home I lived in. The living room and all the rooms were deco-rated perfectly to my taste; however, I did not have a separate family room, which I deeply wanted. One day while driving through my neighborhood I saw a house for sale. I went in to inquire about it and the owner was an old man preparing to go into an assisted living home. Eventually, my offer was accepted to buy the home. I put my house up for sale on a Wednesday and had an open house the following Saturday. During the open house, I received multiple offers. For the next few weeks after that, I would go by the new house to look at it and imagine where I would place my furniture. During my visits, I would talk with him about his life, and we became fast friends. The house had a pool and a beau-tiful view from the living room; however, it did not have a separate family room. I let that go because the view of the pool was so beautiful. On the seventeenth day, He informed me he did not want to sell the house to me. He stated he wanted to die in the house because his wife had died there. Despite his kind gesture of presenting me with a beautiful chess set, I was left in a difficult position as I had already sold my home and needed to find a new one ASAP. After consulting with legal and real estate professionals, it became apparent that pursuing the purchase of the home would be a lengthy process, and I ultimately decided to move on. I changed realtors and frantically started looking for another home. I found a second home but lost the bid because the new realtor failed to respond to the counteroffer in time. The buyers of my home experienced complications and required additional time, this ultimately benefited me since I was still searching for a suitable home. Shortly thereafter, I connected with my real estate agent and discovered a home that met all my specifications. There was strong competition from other offers; therefore, I presented my offer with a letter highlighting my status as a single working individual who also cares for foster children and expressed how the layout of the house with three rooms on one side, a master on the other, a separate family room connected to the kitchen, and proximity to local schools made it ideal. Fortunately, my offer was accepted.

Several weeks after moving in, I learned that the seller of the initial property had sold it to someone else. However, I am grateful to the old wise man for acting on his intuition and deciding not to sell the home to me, as he believed or somehow knew it was not the right fit.

My new house turned out to be the perfect home to continue fostering in, which I did for the next several years before eventually adopting a baby girl. Her adoption story is another miracle story for another book. However, down the street from my new home, which was located on a peaceful court, was a home daycare/afterschool care run by a loving family that my daughter attended until middle school. My daughter is now a teenager, and the daycare has closed, but the family have become her god-grandparents and are an essential part of our lives. It's amazing to think about how different life could have been if I hadn't ended up at this house. It's also a powerful reminder that there are greater forces at work, even when we don't realize it.

If we remain grateful for everything (the good, the bad, and the ugly), and allow ourselves to be led by the Spirit, we will always end up in a good place. Just stay in the flow and let the Universe Provide.

Albert Einstein

"Don't wait for miracles, your whole life is a miracle."

CHAPTER 2
The Universe Knows the Way

OWNER & FOUNDER OF CONSCIOUS LIFE
INSTITUTE
SHIRLEY RYAN, PHD, CCHT

MANY PEOPLE THINK of the Law of Attraction when they want things, money, and abundant lifestyles. However, abundance is way more than the notion of getting nice things into your life. How happy are you when you have had a day where everything goes the way you want it to, everything just feels right? Everything moves easily and effortlessly. Relationships feel good. The world looks wonderful… Nice huh? That said, I do understand that money and things are icing on the cake, which is at the forefront of people's minds, so I'll begin to paint a picture by relating a personal story to help you understand.

Some years ago, we decided to downsize, move, and live a simpler life as we eased into retirement over the next 10 years or so. We looked at and thought about what that would look like. On some levels, times were dictating a direction, but on another level, we went in full agreement with the decision to simplify. One thing I never do, however, is let go of beauty and nature. So, we wanted "simple" yes, but it had to fit my aesthetic needs as well. I've enlisted the aid of the Universe over the past 38 years on 4 different occasions to find a perfect home, consciously or unconsciously of the process.

A tall order, but nothing is too hard for the Universe and that is when we put the Law of Attraction to work. This last couple of times, we were the most directive as we went house hunting. Where did we want to live and what would the house and area look like? The house had to be all on one level, at least a couple thousand sq. ft., overlooking the water, fit around our budget, and be in a warm climate within driving distance of my family!

We found the perfect house twice. The long and the short of it was the first house (the perfect one) was bid out in a day at 80K over the asking price. Then we found the second house some months later, (almost perfect) and fell through too. I sat wondering what to do next. I knew I was working too hard…Let go I thought to myself. My thoughts drifted to all that I know about the Law of the Universe and my thinking style. Remember, feelings also make a difference; therefore, you can't think positive thoughts and feel differently, (angry, sad, depressed) or anything like that, right? If you are in a relationship, then both of you must be on the same page. Oh yes, and a big part of it is the belief that what you want will come to you, and then allowing it in. When you are frustrated, relax, and realize that timing is also important. We had sold our house and had to move, so there was some impatience to get going. I relaxed, timing is everything I said to myself, remember?

My next move was to say (and especially to believe), that the right place will come, and *the Universe knows the way*—my job is to get out of the way! And I did... A few days later I was on Craigslist looking at options for homes, we decided we would rent for a couple of years, not sure where we wanted to live forever... there it was again, not "a" perfect home, "the" perfect home! Our first choice was on the market as a rental! Not only was it there as a rental, but the only flaw was an old kitchen, and it was remodeled to our taste, down to the kind of granite we would have chosen in the kitchen! (See the "timing" was the owners were busy remodeling to our taste on their dime!) We rented this lovely 2500 sq. ft. home on a large, intercity lake at a price we could afford. I live in gratitude to the Universe; for all that I have in life, and I want you all to have these things too, and more!

This may be too political, but here is one - the request is implied:

Nourishment of Another Kind: Yesterday I drove to my daughter's house to spend the afternoon with her, to hug, to be, and to nourish each other. On the return trip, there was unusually heavy traffic, so I sat on the freeway which had now become a "parking lot." As I sat there, I looked up at a familiar landmark that I had watched over the years. First a simple outline with white rocks on the edge of a gently sloping hillside. Now, years later, it was outlined and sparkling with a white rope light that edged the huge cross: Jesus Saves written in the middle. Because the hillside was so dark, all that was visible was the cross floating there in the darkness, seemingly floating above the ground just slightly tipped forward to see the writing. I smiled to myself in recognition of this powerful message and turned my eyes back to the road, and the car edged another inch or two forward.

My eyes are tired, I thought, and they burned a bit, so I decided to put on some music to wake myself up. I was wearing a mobile wireless earbud that was hooked together in the back. I had used it to talk with my sister earlier, leaving it on in case I had a call. In the darkness I struggled to find my iPhone to put some music on, wondering which piece of music would energize me. I rarely listen to the hundreds I've collected over the years, preferring to turn on Pandora to one of my stations. Then something wonderful happened, music started playing automatically. The song: The Lord's Prayer, I didn't know that I had this recording by Susan Boyle. Next came "Let There Be Peace on Earth"; (and let it begin with me...); which was played twice by different artists. Next came: The Miracle of the Candle, This Old Cross, and a flood of Christmas music. Music played for an hour, some songs repeating themselves. Then the music stopped as abruptly as it began.

I sat in the quiet of my car, now driving at a normal speed. I felt a rush of gratitude and peace as I recounted the experience, hoping not to forget a moment of it. What did all this mean? It will mean different things to different people. For me it meant that we are not alone, we have the strength of the Universe at our backs, and we are far more powerful than we know. Let me say that even though the opportunity of a moment came in the form of a cross, symbolically, the meaning for me was to get off the cross and stand for what you believe in, and what you want to see happen! We are in this together and we don't have to let "authoritarianism" win today. We don't have to let another Hitler-like personality rule the country.

We can stand in peaceful unity, stronger together, watchful, and confident that we have the tools to make a difference. Now more than ever, we must stay focused and alert, keep our energy high, and see only what we want to happen. In other words, stay out of fear. The energy of love matters more than ever. Be at peace in this, we are not alone! I am grateful. If vision boards and other techniques of the Law of Attraction haven't worked for you, this method might be helpful. This method works for money flow, relationships, job, or career enhancements, and just about anything. Let's look at a small medical problem.

I shared that I had a bacterial infection in my ear, which quickly blocked my ears so I could not hear. The placebo effect wasn't working for various reasons. I decided to try this easy-peasy method. I asked for a return to hearing: 'I hear perfectly' was the request and I immediately could hear, the process started after 10 minutes, and by 2 hours, full success. That said, I didn't get a full resolution. I noticed a crackly sound, probably fluid buildup in the inner ear. I could hear well enough now to know I had to do an additional 2-cup method.

I looked for just the right wording yesterday, getting suggestions from my daughter as I was visiting her. Well, I came home, went to bed and this morning my ears were cleared. I didn't need the method because I had already activated the placebo effect. That is the part of us that can connect with our brain chemistry to release the chemicals stored to heal any medical issue we have. We are limitless.

So, think this through. If beliefs are wavering or you feel so bad that you can't connect with your inner healer, think of what a small part of the desire looks like. Focus on it, apply the method, and see how you might realize part of what you want. Then you can build from there with another (small) dimensional jump. It may help to realize that there is a dimension in which you have exactly what you want. Your objective is to get there.

The 2 Cup Manifestation Method

Isaiah 55:11

"So shall my word be that goes out from my mouth, it shall not return to me empty, but it shall accomplish that which I purpose, and shall succeed in the thing for which I sent it."

CHAPTER 3
I Was Born For This!

KEYNOTE SPEAKER, LIFE COACH, WELLNESS
ADVOCATE, AUTHOR - FOUNDER OF "WOMEN ON
THE GROW" 501C3
JEWEL DIAMOND TAYLOR

IN 1984 I began to hear my first motivational messages from speakers like Jim Rohn, Les Brown, and Terry Cole-Whitaker. After working several jobs believing I was just passing through, these speakers lit a fire in my soul. That fire still burns to this day (2024).

I don't know if I had blind faith, courage, audacity, or just knew in my bones that I was born to be a positive difference maker.

My jobs in the aerospace industry, a local hospital, the sheriff's department, the city hall, and countless temp jobs paid the bills, but they didn't light me up. However, at 34 years of age with two young boys and a husband who thought I had lost my mind, I set in motion a goal to find a part-time job and began my local speaking career. I could see in my mind's eye me holding a microphone and speaking to the audience. I could feel the excitement, optimism, and full_thrill_ment of audiences responding to my messages. I felt like a big door was opening for me and with no mentors, sponsors, website, speaking experience, or map… I took a leap of faith. I downsized my lifestyle. I knew it would take time to build up my income and grow from free to fee as an inspirational speaker. My clear intention was to find a part-time job close to home so I could see my two sons off to school in the morning and be home when they returned home after school. My vision was to be near nice restaurants so I could meet women for one-on-one counseling/coaching sessions to impart my passion and tips about goal setting. I didn't wait until I had an office. I didn't wait until someone permitted me to start. My spirit said, **"YES, I was born for this."**

I set a clear goal to quit my secure job by January 1986. The momentum happened quickly. I found part-time employment working for an amazing female entrepreneur 10 minutes from home with the perfect hours.

The following poem has special meaning to me. It was given to me in December 1985 by a co-worker when I decided to quit my job in aerospace to pursue my goal as a professional speaker.

Your life lies as a panorama unfolding before you.
Ahead there are mountains and valleys
Deserts, oceans, and meadows.
And the roads… the choices
Are many;
And their ends… the results,
Are often distant and varied.

There might come happiness or sorrow;
Mere contentment or total fulfillment;
Exultation or regret.
But always,
Until one has reached the
Height of his or her aspirations,
There must be change.

Choose your roads carefully.
Be cautious and analytical;
And free and flexible
Within yourself.
Try to anticipate all that might lie ahead,
And if your choice happens to lead to something less
Than what was expected, feel not too
Discouraged, remorseful, or defeated.
Leave it and choose another.
For through experience,
One's knowledge does usually broaden;
And often,
The second road is far more promising than could have been the
first.

Maintain hope, confidence, and resolution,
And remember always;
That he who stays within a desert
When he yearns for the sea,
Grows gradually deeper in
Frustration and regret,
And in the end, perishes-
Having hardly lived at all.

I was in a desert (unfulfilled career) and I was yearning for the sea. I left my comfort zone in 1986, followed my bliss, set my goals, charted my course, and coped with many (valleys) and unexpected personal, professional, and financial challenges. But I have also been on many mountain tops.

This poem was a gift and a blessing to me because I experienced resistance, resentment, and fear when I decided to take a new road and leave my desert of frustration. This poem motivated me to not look back. I share it with you now in hopes it will inspire you to not allow new opportunities to pass you by. LIFE is full of "If's".

I began speaking for many local organizations in my southern California area (e.g. schools, YWCA, churches, community building events, etc.) As my resume gained momentum, I began to receive invitations simply by word of mouth and I would think to myself… "I am a national motivational speaker" even though I hadn't left the state.

In hindsight, I realize I was tapping into the Isaiah 55:11 scripture which says, "So shall my word be that goes out from my mouth, it shall not return to me empty, but it shall accomplish that which I purpose, and shall succeed in the thing for which I sent it."

My invitations started coming nationwide and have been invited as a paid speaker for 35 of the 50 states (e.g. many government agencies, corporations, universities, women's conferences, churches, book signings, retreats, and women's recovery organizations). I was a speaker for the African American Women on Tour Conference for 12 years. I was the conference mistress of ceremonies introducing iconic women like **Susan Taylor, Dr. Maya Angelou, Coretta Scott King, Dr. Shirley Caesar, Iyanla Vanzant, Lynn Whitfield, Johnnetta Cole, Frances Cress Welsing, Nikki Giovanni, Alice Walker, Sonia Sanchez, Mae Jemison, Debbie Allen, and so many more.**

I began to upgrade my thoughts. My faith, worthiness, networking, confidence, reputation, and resume continued to grow. In the early 90's I started telling myself, "I am an international speaker." I didn't even have a passport. My thoughts did not return empty. I truly believe my thoughts, words, feelings, and the grace of God opened more doors. I am a manifester. I am an author. I am a life coach and counselor. I am an in-demand inspirational speaker. I speak what I want to SEE. I believe it before I see it. I am empowered to accomplish what I speak about, think about, and act upon.

I got my passport and the invitations started to happen. I have been truly blessed to meet amazing event hosts and speak into the lives of countless men and women in Turks and Caicos, the Bahamas, Jamaica, St. Kitts, Brazil, London, Cancun, Norway, the

Virgin Islands, and host my first Women on the Grow conference in South Africa.

I knew my words, thoughts, feelings, actions, and faith had the power to manifest what I was focusing on from local to national to international speaking engagements. I kept the main thing… the MAIN THING even in times of disappointments, cancellations, little checks, no checks, bad checks, surgery, financial ups and downs, the loss of my mother to cancer and my 38-year-old son losing his battle to cancer and pivoting through the historical pandemic.

The anointing, passion, and fire still keep me going and pouring into so many lives. After 35+ years of speaking, teaching, traveling, and balancing my family life as a wife, mother, and grandmother and Founder of a wonderful non-profit organization to empower women living in hardship "Women on the Grow, Inc. 501c3"… I am still inspired to press on. As long as I have my health, I intend to keep the main thing… the MAIN THING. I was born for this! I pray my story will inspire someone who is waiting, doubting, hesitating, or distracted to understand the power of what they see, believe, think, and speak can happen. Take steps to trust and grow in the process of the promise over your life.

Email: JewelMotivates@gmail.com

I was
BORN FOR
this

Oprah Winfrey

"Passion is energy. Feel the power that comes from focusing on what excites you."

CHAPTER 4
Follow Your Passion

PHILANTHROPIST, ENTREPRENEUR, AND
SOFTWARE-SOLUTIONS EXECUTIVE.
RAWLVAN R. BENNETT

IN 1980, while in a Los Angeles store, I stumbled upon a magnificent wooden mask from the Democratic Republic of Congo. Little did I know that this chance encounter would mark the beginning of a lifelong journey into the captivating world of African tribal art. The mask, with its intricate details and enigmatic expression, ignited a passionate curiosity in me that I could not ignore. As I collected more pieces over the years, my fascination with African tribal art grew, as did my desire to share this passion with others. I was not content with merely acquiring these treasures; I wanted to bridge the gap between my newfound passion and those who shared the same enthusiasm.

By 2000, I had become a successful executive in the software solutions industry, which allowed me to travel and my trips to Africa were frequent. It was there that I embarked on a transformative journey, delving deeper into the cultures of the tribes and the stories behind their remarkable creations. My travels offered me unparalleled insight into the rich tapestry of African artistry, and I found myself continually drawn to their works.

In 2010, my connection to Africa deepened further as I decided to relocate to Johannesburg, South Africa, where my software company was headquartered. Living there full-time allowed me to immerse myself in the world of African art. I discovered an array of captivating pieces, from wooden masks to statues and bronze warrior sculptures, some standing as tall as five feet, originating from Benin, Nigeria. It was during this time that my fascination with African bronze began to take root. Each piece had a unique story to tell, reflecting the diverse cultures, traditions, and histories of the African continent.

My collection grew to encompass artworks from dozens of tribes and 29 different African countries, including Cameroon, Côte d'Ivoire, Ghana, Mali, Nigeria, Senegal, and the Congo. The pieces ranged in age, with the oldest dating back more than 350 years, and in size and weight, with some towering at 12 feet and weighing up to 700 pounds. These treasures were not mere decorations; they were functional and used for specific purposes within their respective societies.

After years of dedicated collecting, I amassed over 4,000 extraordinary pieces. The desire to share my collection with the world became increasingly urgent, and in March 2017, I fulfilled this dream by opening the Bronze Kingdom Gallery Museum in Southwest Orlando, Florida. Here, I exhibited over 2,000 pieces from my collection, offering visitors a unique experience: the opportunity to touch the artifacts, feel the connection to these ancient cultures, and perhaps even sit on a royal throne. The Bronze Kingdom was not just a place to observe art but a portal to immerse oneself in the traditions, histories, and stories of Africa's diverse peoples.

However, The Bronze Kingdom faced unforeseen challenges as a result of the pandemic of 2019. By 2022, like many businesses, it struggled to weather the storm, and despite my best efforts, it did not survive. Yet, my dream, my passion for African tribal art, and my commitment to sharing these remarkable pieces with the world remain undiminished.

Today, my collection endures, and the stories within each piece continue to inspire and captivate all who have the privilege of encountering them. While the Bronze Kingdom Gallery Museum may have closed its doors, the spirit of discovery and appreciation for the beauty and significance of African tribal art live on, reminding us that art has the power to transcend time and circumstances, connecting us to cultures and stories from across the globe. Dreams never die, my passion continues.

Shaka Zulu - King of the Zulu Nation - South Africa made from Ironwood.

Benin Bronzes from Benin Nigeria - castings of Kings and Queens

41

Bronze Bamoun King and King - seated - from Cameroon

42

Bronze Medicinal piece from Cameroon

Savanah Marble Bust "The Weeping Woman" carved in South Africa by Zimbabwean artist.

Bronze Birthing Scene from Ghana with midwives and King and Queen.

Proverbs 3:5

"Trust in the Lord with all your heart,
and do not lean on your own
understanding."

CHAPTER 5
When God Tells You to Move... MOVE!

SECTION CHIEF, U.S. DEPT. OF AGRICULTURE
BRENDA THOMPSON

I AM a southern California native but currently live in Atlanta, Georgia. I was raised in Compton, California. Attended college in northern California (San Jose State University) and had only left the great state of California to visit Las Vegas, Nevada, and Dallas, Texas. Dallas to escort my niece and nephews back home and Las Vegas for fun with family and friends.

Many people have asked me why I moved to Atlanta. It's hard for me to give them a quick response and some I don't share with because I don't think they would understand the spiritual side of my moving to Georgia. It's not just a one-sentence answer. It took time, trust in God, and faith to make the move.

In 2004, I wanted to take my family on a vacation. I saw advertisements about a TD Jakes MegaFest event being held in Atlanta, Georgia, and for some reason wanted to attend. I had heard so much about Atlanta and wanted to see it and MegaFest was my way of doing it.

My daughter was 15 years old at the time and my son was 13. I kept seeing the MegaFest advertised on TV and hearing it on the radio. I never wanted to attend a MegaFest before, but this one was lying heavy on my mind and heart. My children were excited to go after showing them all the kids and teen programs that were scheduled. Concerts, comedy shows, and learning sessions designed specifically for youth. They grew up attending children's and youth ministries, so this was an opportunity for them to see how it was done at other venues.

My mom had never been to Atlanta before and wanted to go, so she came along too. I could only afford one hotel room so the 4 of us shared 2 queen beds. It was cozy, but we were so excited about the trip, we didn't care and had no problems with the one bathroom. By the end of the day, we were all so tired, we crashed, and it didn't matter that the two of us shared a bed. Needless to say, my Atlanta trip turned out to be life-changing.

When I first arrived at the Georgia Dome, I saw the crowds of people walking and I immediately felt that that I had seen this area before. I had to stop walking and watch things occur and know what the next move would be. I had heard of something called dejà vu but didn't understand it. I experienced this a few times during the first 2 days and I remember saying, "Lord, you showed this to me before, Why?" I kept praying, Lord, what is going on? On about the third day, we had tickets to see Steve Harvey at Phillips Arena. I told them that I felt I needed to attend the church service that evening and could not attend the Steve Harvey comedy show. My kids looked forward to the event, but my mom was too tired and didn't want to attend the show or church service. She decided to stay in the hotel room.

I didn't want to disappoint my kids, but I knew I had to attend the service. My daughter was a remarkable young lady. At 15 she was very responsible and trustworthy. They begged me to let them go and it was something that they were looking forward to. I prayed about it and felt peace about letting them attend. We rode MARTA to Phillips Arena walked them into the arena and identified a meeting spot for them to meet me after the show. I got back on MARTA and went to the Georgia Dome for the service. I knew the Lord was going to speak to me and it was good that I was alone and could focus on the word being spoken.

As TD Jakes started speaking, I started crying. I don't know why. He said that God is opening a door for someone and you must go through that door. He said God is moving you and you must trust him. He said things like God has shown you things and He is moving you. I cried and cried knowing that God was speaking to me. I knew He was moving me to Atlanta. I didn't know why, or how or when. I was to trust Him and be obedient.

After the service, I went to Phillips Arena and met my kids. They were super excited about the show and couldn't wait to tell me everything that was said or happened. I was happy that they enjoyed themselves so much. When we went to the hotel room, I told them and my mom about my experience and how I believed God was moving me to Atlanta. I didn't know how or when, but I knew it was going to happen, and 2 years later… it did!

After living in Atlanta for more than 15 years, I still do not know the why as I'm still growing and learning more about God. He gave me the when and how and I'll briefly share some of the details which ultimately led to the when.

After returning to California, I spoke to a friend and shared my experience. I asked her if she knew anyone in Atlanta that I could talk to. She said that her cousin lived in Atlanta, but she would not give me her number because she didn't want me to leave California. I accepted that because I knew that God was going to move me and I didn't need anyone but Him, but the human side of me wanted to know someone in Atlanta. I let God know all the buts… I know you're moving me, but I don't know anyone there, I don't have any family there, I don't have the money to move, I don't have a job there, and on and on…

A few months later, my friend's cousin came to LA. She visited our church and of course, I spoke to her and told her about my experience, she looked at me and said… "Oh my God" You're the reason. She and her husband felt a heavy desire to come to LA but didn't know why. After I told her my experience, she knew. She told her husband who is a pastor about my experience and they both knew that I was the reason they were to come to LA. I had to scratch off my "but I don't know anyone there."

She invited me to Atlanta, and a couple of months later I visited and just walked through the city to try to get some understanding. God answered all the buts during that visit.

I had lunch with Barbara at the Underground and a friend of hers joined us. Her friend was the Director of Elections for Fulton County. I shared some of my election experience with LA County and she said she had a job opening coming up and would like me to apply. Scratch off the 'but I don't have a job there.'

Barbara and her husband took me around looking at houses. The agent at the model home began talking and she told me she was originally from Bakersfield, California. I told her that I was relocating to Atlanta, and had lots of family in Bakersfield, and started naming a few of them to see if she knew any of them. She stood up with tears in her eyes and said," Those are my cousins too". She said she had been praying for some of her family to move to Atlanta. I didn't even know Terrie. I called a couple of my cousins, and they were amazed too. Terrie was much younger than me, so I didn't remember her until my cousins started placing her. Scratch off the 'but I don't have a family.'

I was stunned, shocked and we all just sat down in amazement. Terrie and I were crying, and Barbara said what more do you need to know that this is confirmation from God?

I didn't need anything else. And two years later, my children and I moved to a suburb in Atlanta, Georgia after my condo in Los Angeles sold in one day. We moved into the same model home where I met my cousin and a week later, I started the job with Fulton County.

God met all my needs. I had no more buts. The "why" continues to grow. I've learned so much. I would have to write a book to convey all the things I have learned.

52

John Mitchell

"Our attitude towards life determines life's attitude towards us."

CHAPTER 6

The D-Attitudes, My Method for Manifesting

AUTHOR, OWNER & PRESIDENT OF I SPEAK!
MICHAEL BRUNDY

I WOULD LIKE to share an event when something I wished for or desired just materialized without any effort on my part, but that is not how my life has worked. I am sure it has happened, but it surely is not the norm. For me and in my life, things have materialized because of my attitude. I have always worked to maintain a positive attitude. I think when we are positive life works better. We can see the bright side of life and see possibilities when we are positive.

Now for me being positive is not just being "pollyannish" and hoping things work out. It's not looking at things that are negative and telling myself, they are positive. Being positive is looking at possibilities and then doing what must be done to make them a reality.

I have a proven method for this. I call the method the D-Attitudes. I say D-Attitudes because I can think of so many words that begin with "d" that describe the necessary attitude needed to succeed. Words like – discipline, determination, desire, development, dependable, dogged.

But my favorite D-words are **Decide, Declare, Do and Delight**. These words represent my four-step method to success. I've used this in my own life and shared it with others and it works.

The first D is for Decide. We must first always decide what it is we want. We must know where we want to go. We must know what we want to do.

If we don't know what we want, we can't make any plans for manifestation. If we don't know where we want to go how can we know the correct direction or the correct first step? The first thing anyone must do if they want to manifest in their lives is decide what it is that they want.

The second D is for Declare. I think there is power in making declarations. A declaration is not a question. It is a statement.

When we make declarations, we tell others and the universe what it is that we want. When we tell others what we want, they may offer us help or suggestions. Even if they are negative about our declarations, we can use that as motivation to see it through. But more importantly, when we make declarations, we are telling ourselves what we want and what we are committed to.

There is power in making declarations out loud, even making them in front of others who may ridicule you or not see it as a possibility. Those people can be your inspiration and the reason to keep chasing your dream.

For example, if you declare to your friends that you are going to lose weight and eat healthier, they will be watching you. When they see you reach for that second donut you can bet, they will speak up. They will question you, tease you, and keep you on your goal.

The third D is for Doing. You simply must do the hard work. Faith without action is dead. We must move our feet to reach our goal. No matter how well we plan, visualize, dream or wish, we must eventually take action. That's the doing. It may not be easy to do the whole project at one time, but we can always break things into smaller pieces. That's how you get things done. You must work.

The fourth D is for Delight. I think it is important to delight in our accomplishments. We need to take time to pat ourselves on the back when we have completed our goal.

During this time, we not only complement ourselves for our success but reevaluate our activity. What did we do well, and what can we improve on? What lessons did we learn?

It's important to feel the success as well as critique our success. This is how we delight in the process and prepare for the next goal. This is how we manifest what we want.

I've used the D-Attitudes, the 4-D method in my own life many times.

Years ago, I decided that I wanted to run a marathon. A marathon is a 26.2-mile race. It is a big deal, a big goal.

After I decided to run the race. I made declarations. I signed up for the race, paid the fee, and began to tell others that I was going to be working out so I could run a marathon.

You can bet my friends and family began to watch me. They watched what I ate. They asked if I had worked out. They asked about my progress. They stayed with me about my training. And if I was coming up short, they were sure to tell me. They were my fuel.

When the big day came, I ran and completed the 26.2-mile race. I've run several since then. I always delight in that accomplishment. I have my medals hanging in my closet as inspiration. I have photographs of me crossing the finish line. Whenever I'm challenged, I remember that I am a marathoner and that gets me through.

I enjoy the Delight stage but know that there is always another race, another challenge.

This 4-D Method is my way of manifesting. I believe in cause and effect. I can be the cause and I can be the effect. When I practice this method, I'm doing just that.

I wish things did just happen for me, that my dreams would just magically appear. But that hasn't been my reality. Even when I'm not consciously practicing my 4-Ds I know that my thoughts, my efforts, and my perseverance are what works for me. It's about my attitude.

I think this is true for everyone. Sometimes it may seem as if things just happen. But there is always a cause behind each effect. I think we are always able to manifest what we want if we remember cause and effect and use the D-Attitudes. I encourage you to decide what you want, make declarations, set goals, do the hard work, and then delight in your accomplishments. It worked for me; it will work for you.

58

Francis Bacon

"A wise man will make more opportunities than he finds."

CHAPTER 7

A Truly 'Oz' Moment

CEO AND FOUNDER AT ENTHRONE RECORDS ENT. LLC

ANDRÉ PITTMON

I DRAW inspiration from my experiences at Hollywood High, USC, and the Warner Bros. Studios' work-educational program. A journey that has attracted a slew of rich career opportunities. I also praise my mentor Barry Reardon, former President of Sales and Distribution, (recently deceased), for the guidance and patience to help me develop my professional skills. We collaborated on many films: *Superman, Twister, Pelican Brief, The Green Mile, The Perfect Storm*, and the 1st edition of *The Color Purple*.

The moment that altered my life was as a student at Hollywood High. Initially not impressed by the option until I learned I could leave school at 10 a.m. to participate. The first time, as an 18-year-old, I stepped foot on the Warner Bros. Studios lot, I was transformed.

It was as if, like Dorothy, when she opened the door after the farmhouse crashed, the scene changed from sepia to full color… that's how I felt. I strolled about the lot in awe of the spectacle, peeping in and out of windows and doorways, when, to my shock, I saw Bette Davis eating in the canteen. I truly was in OZ and I've never been the same. The knowledge of working in a major studio is priceless.

Another major observation I learned from personal experience is knowing and embracing opportunities.

Prospects come in all shapes and sizes, not always black or white… something you'd never think of as an opportunity might lead you to the manifestation you've prayed for.

Be vigilant and ready for the surprises that life brings to you.

One afternoon at work, I was called into my boss's office. I feared a reprimand. When I entered, there stood Spike Lee. My boss introduced me as the publicist assigned to work on the film *Malcolm X*. I looked at my boss like… what are you talking about? It turned out that I was the only person of color on the lot at the time. Spike insisted on collaborating with someone of ethnic heritage. I accepted the challenge and excelled.

While the Warner Bros. experience was a blessing on many fronts, it was a stepping stone. My greatest dream was to be involved in the music industry at the top level. To make a difference in the quality and inclusivity of music… not only for me but for my fellow musical and artistic comrades. The career of a lifetime is what I asked for and the universe delivered.

Based in Los Angeles, CA, credited as an international influencer in the music, TV, and film industry, André Pittmon, CEO and

Founder at Enthrone Records Ent. LLC has forged a path through a complex, diverse, yet unwavering trek forward to success.

Since 2017, he has commanded a record company fashioned to support artists, and musicians, pledging or seasoned, to attract and embrace their rights of accomplishment and recognition as creative, spiritual forces.

To date, Enthrone is proud to announce the release of Lattice Lawrence's new single "Taking It Back," and Pat Hodges, formerly with Motown's Hodges, James & Smith, and her latest release, "Love Revolution." Also, Prophet Michael's single, "God is On Fire." The innovative list of artists and record releases from the studio continues to grow.

Proverbs 16:9

"A man's heart deviseth his way: but the
LORD directeth his steps."

CHAPTER 8

My Unseen Conversion

UNIVERSITY PASTOR, DIRECTOR OF CHURCH
RELATIONS AT VIRGINIA UNION UNIVERSITY

REV. DR. ANGELO V. CHATMON

IT WAS MARCH 4, 1974. I found myself sitting in an Assemblies of God Church in Yankton, South Dakota. It was more than an anomaly that I was in South Dakota, having traveled by car there from Los Angeles, California in 1972. What a contrast of cities.

Up until my arrival, most Southern Californians thought that South Dakota was somewhere down south. Somewhere between Mississippi and Georgia. However, my tenure in this obscure town is a story for another time. But in this obscure town, my unseen conversion occurred. It was a Sunday afternoon service on the date aforementioned. I, and four other college students had been invited by 'Michael T', a recently converted weed-smoker and basketball player, to attend a church service. It took months for 'Michael T.' to recruit me to church. He would knock on my door every Sunday morning with an invitation. However, I turned him down for weeks. Nevertheless, he kept badgering me, saying that "God was trying to get my attention".

I finally compromised to attend a service of my choosing if he,

'Michael T.', would stop knocking on my door on Sunday mornings. Sometime later he invited me and five other students to attend a service that featured the testimonies of young adults who had given their lives to Christ.

On the evening of March 4, 1974, I attended that service. We arrived and took our seats in the sanctuary. I admit to feeling a little out of sorts because it was the first time in my life I had ever been in a church where the parishioners were primarily white. I was not accustomed to their music, their preaching, nor the testimonials of this traveling band of evangelists, who were former runaways, drug addicts, and societal non-conformists until divine intervention intervened. That was the outcome of everyone's story. Storylines that, as I was sitting there, did not interest me. I was sitting there but my mind was far away in other thoughts until…. until I caught the gaze of the man on the drums.

A man was sitting on the drums staring directly at me. How long he had been there, I don't recall. As far as I know, he had been accompanying the worship music. Before I took notice of him, his drumming had no relevance. But now I see him and he's staring at me. He is staring! Staring directly at me! His stare is not accidental, it was intentional!

I tested the intentionality of his stare by looking away from him and then looking back. His gaze would still be upon me! To detour him from his glaze, I gave him a menacing stare back, as if to say, "You'd better stop staring at me"! He was not intimidated and continued to stare. He kept his eyes on me until the service ended.

After the benediction was given, something within me said, get out of here as quickly as you can! As I proceeded to get to the end of the pew, the man on the drums walked over to me. He caught me before I could get away. He placed his right hand upon my left shoulder and said, "The Lord has need of you". Then he preceded to utter some prophecy about me that I cannot recall due to my displeasure with him. But at the end of his statement, he said, "For you, the climb will be very hard, but when you reach the top of the mountain you will see the purple rose", (Glory to God). Then he asked me, "Do you accept Christ as your savior?" I intended to say no, but yes came out of my mouth. Suddenly, I had a moment of exhilaration. Something was changing instantly in my body and my mind. And as I stood there in a daze, my college friends came over to me to ask why I was standing and looking the way I was. So, I shared with them what had happened between me and the man on the drums. The response was, "What man on the drums?"

That night, I was brought to Christ by a man no one else saw. When I returned to my dormitory room, I accepted my call to the ministry. Upon the writing of this story in 2023, I have been in the pastoral ministry for over 40 years. Later on, in their lives, three of the other students came into the ministry as well. However, mine was an unseen conversion.

Mark 11:24

"Therefore I say unto you, What things soever ye desire, when ye Pray, believe that ye receive them, and ye shall have them."

CHAPTER 9
Breathe, Believe and Receive

AUTHOR, ENTREPRENEUR
CARLA SPARKS

THE OUTSIDE PERIMETER of my home is surrounded by a variety of beautiful plants, flowers, and palm trees. Fresh air, blue skies, butterflies, birds and bees, sweet aromas, and a water fountain enhance the peaceful environment. Looking at my lovely garden reminds me of the wonders of nature and the majestic splendor of the universe. I believe miracles occur daily, they may not be earth-shattering, but each blessing that manifests in my life strengthens my belief in a higher power. I can recall countless times when I said what I said, and the universe provided.

The story I wish to share goes like this. I closed escrow on my home in November 2005, the day before Thanksgiving. When I moved in the following month, the exterior grounds consisted of dirt which is common with new construction. According to the Homeowner Association guidelines, it was my responsibility to landscape the property within a year. The first year, I was strapped for cash and exceeded the deadline. Several of my neighbors hired a landscaping company that did an outstanding job. Even though I wasn't ready to get the actual work done, I scheduled an appointment for an estimate.

As I ripped pages from magazines and purchased a tropical landscaping book, I was dreaming of Caribbean vibrations. The company attached a ten-thousand-dollar price tag to my vision. The owner explained it was a slow season; as Spring approached, he would get busier, and the cost of supplies would increase. He was willing to accept a small down payment and monthly payments, but I didn't want to increase my monthly bills. However, I was tired of looking at dirt, plus I was in jeopardy of paying a fine. I took funds that were designated towards other financial obligations to piece together three thousand dollars to greenlight the project. When the crew began working, I said to myself I'm not going to stress; someway, somehow, I will pay the balance.

Four days later, I looked in my mailbox and discovered an envelope that contained a check for nearly four thousand dollars. I smiled, looked up, and thanked God. It turns out, that I had refinanced an investment property two years prior, the company was audited and discovered they had overcharged in closing costs. The landscaper blessed me with a kind gesture, he took me to the wholesale nursery and allowed me to purchase the palm trees at cost on my credit card. In total, the holy spirit showed up and showed out supplying my needs to the tune of fifty-four hundred dollars. I paid the invoice in full over the next three months. Hallelujah!

My outdoor space is my happy place, it's the gift that keeps on giving. Time has passed and the palm trees have grown as high as my house. When I look outside, the tropical greenery provides stunning visuals from seven rooms. The moral of the story is when life deals you dirt, be mindful of the seeds you plant, commit to caring for them, and cultivate your faith to increase the odds of ending up with a beautiful garden.

Jeremiah 29:11

"For I know the plans I have for you."
Declares the Lord, "plans to prosper you
and not to harm you, plans to give you
hope and a future."

CHAPTER 10
When Rainstorms (and Traffic Jams) Open Doors

PRINCIPLE LEAD RECRUITER
MARTIN L. HOWARD II

2019. That was the last normal year for my family. At the time I didn't know it, but it was. Oh… I'm not talking about Covid and the horrors that came from that the following year, although that is worth mentioning. 2019 was the last year that the core of my immediate family was still intact. It was the last year both of my parents were alive.

March of 2019 found me 15 months in a role I wasn't enthusiastic about, working for a company I wasn't excited about, all while reporting to a manager whom I was less than eager to see daily. The role that had started so positively started to bog me down. What started as a new beginning in a series of new beginnings started to feel like an extended prison sentence. Part of that was due to my personal life at the time. What I kept private from most of my coworkers was that my mom was fighting an aggressive form of cancer that had resurfaced. I had let my manager know and had asked for accommodations that would allow me to spend time with my mom while supporting myself.

Initially, the request was granted with sympathy, empathy, and care, but over time it was met with annoyance and irritation. Meetings that could be done via phone were requested in person (this was before the wide implementation and use of Microsoft Teams and other virtual platforms that would become used during the pandemic). Managers who were used to dropping in without notice to discuss roles and candidates became annoyed when they would come to my office, and I wasn't there. On top of that, I had a coworker acting as a mole or spy for my manager, who took it upon herself to report my whereabouts in the morning and let my manager know that I wasn't in my office right at 9 a.m. That was laughable as I was (and am) a salaried exempt employee. I didn't punch a time clock or record my time. It got to the point that in January my manager pulled me into her office to give me a corrective action notice regarding attendance. When I asked her how she determined if I was or wasn't on time, she advised that she looked in the parking lot for my car since I parked in the same spot; that actually wasn't true, but it was so ridiculous that I just looked at her. I let her know that I don't always park in the same spot, and there were times as I was walking into the building when a manager would see me and want to talk about whatever roles they had going on.

Even with that being said and me reminding her that I was not hourly, and there wasn't a timeclock for me to punch, she was insistent that I needed to "be on time" and that I needed to figure out my personal matters and make more time available in the office. At that point I saw red I reminded her of what the circumstances were. I had hoped to appeal to her humanity since she had lost her mother to cancer, and she of all people should understand what I was experiencing, but that wasn't the case.

Things continued to escalate through January going into February. She would make snide comments about being on time and my commitment to the job. The ironic part in all of this is that, as a recruiter, I was filling my roles sooner than required because I was focused on keeping my workload as light as possible so I could spend time with my mother. Apparently, me doing my job well wasn't enough. For some reason she had it in her head that I was coming in late and nothing I could do would prove otherwise, even me sending emails when I arrived to show that I was there (I didn't do corporate email on my phone then and that's a stance I maintain to this day). Fast forward to mid-February and she calls me into her office again and this time issues me a final warning. If I am "late" one more time she would terminate me. Again, I just looked at her. I asked her how we got to this point, and she told me that we just are, and it is what it is. I walked out of her office annoyed, and extremely irritated. Fast forward to March 6, 2019.

The area I live in had had a mild winter and hadn't had much rain that season. That morning, I woke up at my normal time and got ready. Unbeknownst to me, it was raining a few miles from my home. My drive to work started normally, but as I progressed the rain caught up to where I was, and it started to affect traffic.

8:15 a.m.

Under normal circumstances, the drive to work was 35-45 minutes depending on traffic. At this point, I was about 25 or so miles away. Now I'm stuck on the freeway. Traffic is crawling.

8:20 a.m.

At this point, I have a feeling of dread in the pit of my stomach. Traffic has come to a complete stop. Given where I lived, surface streets would take just as long, if not longer, and would more than likely have heavy traffic from folks leaving the freeway. The rain is coming down and somehow, it's in the same rhythm and syncopation as my heartbeat.

8:35 a.m.

At this point, I've moved maybe a mile or two. There are several accidents as people in the desert don't drive well in the rain. My heart is still beating, and the dread is still there.

8:45 a.m.

I'm a bit further from home, but nowhere near the halfway point to work. Traffic is inching along at a snail's pace.

8:40 a.m.

I send my manager a text directly (not on the group thread that she and my coworkers are on). I let her know that the freeway is a parking lot, and I am braving traffic and on my way. No response from her.

8:50 a.m.

I've moved a bit further, and traffic is incrementally speeding up, but I'm still not at the halfway mark. At this point, I'm facing reality. Unless I can teleport to work like someone from Starfleet or an X-man, the likelihood of me being late for real (ironically) is very high.

9:00 a.m.

As I've been moving along the freeway, I've been watching the clock. However, as the clock ticked and got closer to 9:00, I felt a sense of calm. Once the clock hit 9:00a, as by divine intervention, the freeway opened up and I was able to go to normal speeds again. As I'm driving, I see notifications from the work group chat that multiple people on my team have been delayed by the rain and that they are going to be late. In my mind, at that point, I was tired of my manager and her unrealistic and unreasonable expectations and behavior, and I stopped caring.

9:01 a.m.

I let my manager know that I am still on my way.

Me: I'm still on my way

Sad emoji

Her: Ok

Me: It's a slow-moving parking lot this morning (9:03 a.m.)

Her: Have you made it yet (9:24 a.m.)

Me: I did. Did you get my email? (9:26 a.m.)

Her: Yes, I will talk to you later today (9:50 a.m.)

Me: Ok (9:50 a.m.)

Me: I can start downloading my coworker (9:56 a.m.)

***At this point I've accepted that she is going to stick to her word, regardless of the external circumstances outside of my control, or the fact that more than half of the team was delayed by the weather. ***

Her: Ok. But we still need to meet when I am done with the leadership presentation today (9:57 a.m.)

Me: OK. I'll make my final offers and I'll make sure that all of my requisitions are created and approved or in the process of being (9:58 a.m.)

Her: We still need to talk (9:59 a.m.)

Me: I know. I still have work to do. I'm not going to leave things in a mess though (9:59 a.m.)

Her: Thanks (11:19 a.m.)

During this time, I have let my coworker know that the Manager is going to terminate me for being late. She scoffed and said it wasn't going to happen and that she would be crazy to do so. I let her know that for some reason she wanted to make an example of me and would follow through, so here is my work and the status of everything. As the day progressed my coworker kept asking me if I was sure I was being let go. I kept telling her I was sure I was and to be prepared to absorb my work.

That afternoon she's finally done presenting and she comes into the office. I hear her talking to everyone and making small talk. At that point I'm calm. Surprisingly the rain that was coming down like cats and dogs earlier has cleared up and it is absolutely beautiful outside. After a time she finally pops her head in my office and says that we need to talk. My coworker looks at me and I look back at her. My manager and I walked to her office.

She proceeds to give the standard HR speech and after going on for far too long, in my opinion, she gives me the keys to my handcuffs and lets me know that she is separating our employment. While I was calm earlier and had felt a sense of peace, at that moment I felt a great weight lifted off me. At that moment I knew everything would be ok. I didn't know how things would be ok, but knowing the God I serve, and how he has been there for me in the past, I knew I would be fine.

The next day I traveled to my parent's home and spent time with my mom through the weekend. I was able to spend additional time with her that wouldn't have been possible with my current job, and I was so grateful. As my mom's condition grew more serious, due to my being out of work, I was able to spend more time with her during the week along with my other siblings.

Fast forward to May of 2019. I was offered a job with my current company as a contractor. The salary was more than what I was making at my previous job, but the biggest draw to the role was that it was automatically remote. I was working from home!! I would be able to support myself while spending precious time with my mom. And that is what I did. Because one door closed, another opened that allowed me to spend time with the person I loved the most in this world. Sadly, in October of that year, my mom's fight with cancer ended. The next month, I turned 40, and we had our first series of holidays without her and celebrated as a family of five. New Year 2020 comes, and then…Covid hit. The world as we knew it shut down. Businesses closed their doors. Companies laid people off. Toilet paper and paper towels were being brought at rates never seen. Store shelves were empty. It was eerie. However, God set me up in such a way that my remote job was still remote, and because I work in healthcare, it was still business as usual.

What was meant for downfall was ultimately the event that allowed one door to close for me to walk through another one.

Four years later, there have been other losses. My siblings and I are now a family of four as our father unexpectedly passed away in January 2022. No warning. No sickness. Here one Friday and gone the following Thursday. But I'm still standing in God's promises. My parents were Christians who were strong in their faith. They gave each of us a foundation that has kept us standing strong, even in the roughest of storms. Prior to it becoming super popular and mainstream, the Bible scripture that my mom claimed for me in my late teens was Jeremiah 29:11 - For I know the plans I have for you," declares the Lord, "plans to prosper you and not to harm you, plans to give you hope and a future.

Even before I knew I needed it, God was working for my good. He foresaw a situation and event that could have been catastrophic and allowed it to be used for my good immediately and long term. For this blessing and many others, I am so grateful. He's always known what I needed before I knew it, and because of this, my faith and trust continue to grow each day. As Proverbs 3:5-6 states: Trust in the Lord with all your heart, and do not lean on your understanding. In all your ways acknowledge Him, and He will make straight your paths. Trust and faith are easy to talk about when the skies are clear, and trouble isn't at your door. The true test of our faith is demonstrating that trust in God even when we don't know the next move. Faith is trusting even when we don't know how the door will open, or if we have to climb through a window. As I look back on my life and see how God has worked, I am grateful for the tough times. I'm grateful for the unknown. I'm grateful for the spy that God allowed to set things in motion. Had it not been for those actions, who knows how the story would have gone? As you look back, thank God for the journey that allowed you to make it to your destination. The paths, twists, and turns were for your good. The next time it rains, remember the promises that were made all those years ago. Storms aren't always pleasant, but in some cases, they can open doors.

Romans 8:28

"And we know that all things work together for good to them that love God, to them who are the called according to his purpose."

CHAPTER 11

Fulfilling Your Life Calling

EXECUTIVE PASTOR - ST PAUL MISSIONARY BAPTIST CHURCH, SACRAMENTO CA
LAMONT HARRIS

AS A CHILD, I grew up attending and participating in church regularly. My parents were very involved in church, so I had a first-hand view of church life. I had an opportunity to sit in leadership meetings and observe how things operated. In the summer the youth were allowed to serve in various leadership roles and attend leadership meetings.

I have always been a people person and knew I wanted to help people, so when it was time to declare a major in college, I decided on Social Work. As I took classes, I began to see how what I was learning applied to the church. As an example, in a Long-Range Planning (now known as strategic planning) class, I learned about identifying a mission, goals and objectives, strategies, measurable results, and evaluation. When I took a statistics class, I thought about why not use empirical data to make decisions (now known as Data-Driven Decision-Making) instead of feelings, family relationships, or politics. In a community development class, I was convinced that the church should be involved in the transformation of communities (this is now known as the Community Development and Social Justice Ministry).

As early as my sophomore year, I sensed a calling on my life, however, I was clear it was not a calling to be a preacher, so I decided I was going to be a good Christian social worker. After completing my Junior year, that summer when I went home, I met with my Pastor, Dr. Manuel Scott, Sr., and told him, I felt this calling in my life, but I knew it was not to be a preacher. His response was classic. "Lamont, the problem with the black church is everyone thinks if someone knows the word if they are a good speaker, they should be a preacher. In our tradition, we only value the Pastor, but we need other staff to get the work done. The white church understands that they hire staff." He went on to say, "Be prayerful and faithful and God will allow you to exercise your gifts." I left the meeting knowing I was not called to be a preacher, and as far as I knew most churches had a secretary and custodian, and I knew I did not want to be either of those.

That summer when I returned to school, my pastor, Dr. Ephraim Williams, asked me, "What are you going to do when you graduate?" I said, "I plan to go to Graduate School and work on a master's in social work. If I don't get into Graduate School, I will try to find a job, if I don't find a job, I will go back home to LA." He said, "For three years I have been praying for someone to help me, and the Lord keeps giving me your name. Would you be interested in working with me when you finish school? I said, "Yes, exactly what would I be doing?" He said, "Helping with the business operations and administration of the church." His response was an answer to my prayer. I had been praying for three years that God would show me his will for my life. I knew there was a calling on my life, but I thought it would be limited to being a good Christian Social Worker. Interestingly enough, in confidence, Dr. Williams asked three of the church mothers to pray for someone to help him. All three had the same response, with the same words, "What about that young man that goes to College here?" Over the same three-year period, in which I was seeking God's will for my life, my Pastor and three church mothers were praying.

I was admitted to Graduate School. In my first year, I had a student internship working for the California State Assembly Committee on Aging. The first hearing I attended; the Assemblyman was confronting a State Agency that misappropriated funds for a food program. He told them, "Go back, find that money, and report back to this committee." At the next meeting, that agency reported they found the money. I walked out of that meeting thinking, that's what the church needed to be doing, advocating for the underrepresented people in our society. This was further confirmation, that through the church I could do advocacy and community impact work just as I had learned in the school of Social Work.

Once I completed Grad School, Dr. Williams asked me if I was still interested. I said, "Yes." This was in May, I started working at the church in January of the next year, and I have been working there fulfilling my life's calling for 41 years.

Proverbs 3:6

"In all thy ways acknowledge him, and he shall direct thy paths."

CHAPTER 12
Over Coming Insecurities

OWNER - REALTOR, AUTHOR, AND AN AWARD-
WINNING ENTREPRENEUR
MARQUETTA DEVILLE

GROWING UP, I faced the challenge of being placed in a reading improvement class. Although it was only for one year, the experience left a lifelong effect on me. The constant embarrassment of having my name called out in front of everyone made me feel insecure and worried about what people thought of me. Despite my accomplishments, I was still struggling with insecurities and a lack of self-worth.

However, in December 2021, I attended a conference that changed my life. During a breakout session, I was able to see myself in a new light and realize my true calling. I committed to God that if He provided me with a financial blessing, I would run in the fullness of who He created me to be and never look back.

Four days after returning from the conference, I received a grant that allowed me to launch the Wealth Mindset Brunch series. As each event sold out, I continued to pursue my calling by taking platform training courses, writing my first book, finishing my associate degree, and partnering with my husband for the Wealth

Mindset Conference Las Vegas a sold-out event with over 200 in attendance. Today I am the co-owner of DeVille Realty Group, in Henderson Nevada, and is Nevada's Largest Black Owned Real Estate company.

My story serves as a reminder that the challenges we face in life can either hold us back or propel us forward. It's up to us to decide how we respond to them and whether we will allow them to define us. With determination and a willingness to step out of our comfort zones, we can overcome our insecurities and reach our full potential.

Samuel 3:10

"Speak, for your servant is listening."

CHAPTER 13

Just Stop

HOLISTIC LIVING AND WELLNESS EXPERT,
PRODUCER, TALK SHOW HOST, PUBLISHED
AUTHOR

LYNNIS WOODS-MULLINS CHHC, CLC, CPI

FOR MANY YEARS, I believed that success required relentless hard work. I worked long hours, pushing myself to the brink in the hopes of achieving my goals. I believed that if I just worked hard enough, I could make anything happen.

However, as I approached my 60th birthday, I began to feel a sense of restlessness. Despite all my hard work, I couldn't seem to take my business to the next level. I knew that something had to change, but I wasn't sure what.

That's when I started hearing the voice in my head - the one that kept telling me to "just stop." At first, I ignored it. After all, how could I "just stop" when there was so much work to be done?

But the voice persisted, and eventually, I had no choice but to listen. After twisting my ankle during a walk, I was forced to take a break. I was anxious about all the work I was missing out on, but I was in too much pain to do anything else.

As I rested, something shifted. It was as though the universe was waiting for me to "just stop" before it could shower me with blessings. Potential clients called, money came into my account, and ideas flowed into my email.

It was a powerful lesson - sometimes, the best thing you can do is to take a step back and let things happen naturally. And as I started to explore the power of "just stop," I realized that there was so much more to it than just taking a break.

I discovered that "just stop" wasn't about giving up on your dreams or abandoning your goals. Instead, it was about letting go of the need to control everything and trusting that the universe had a plan for you.

That didn't mean that I stopped working altogether, of course. Instead, I shifted my approach. I focused on the tasks that truly mattered, rather than just trying to do everything at once. I learned to delegate tasks to others when needed, and I started prioritizing self-care.

It wasn't always easy, of course. Old habits die hard, and it can be difficult to let go of the idea that success requires constant hustle. But as I continued to embrace the power of "just stop," I found that my life and my business started to shift in powerful ways.

I started to experience more joy, more abundance, and more success than ever before. And it wasn't because I was working harder - it was because I was working smarter. By letting go of my need for control and trusting the process, I was able to tap into a greater sense of flow and ease.

Of course, that doesn't mean that I don't work hard anymore. I still put in the effort and the time needed to make things happen. But I do it with a greater sense of ease and a deeper trust in the universe's plan for me.

If you're feeling stuck or restless in your own life or business, I encourage you to explore the power of "just stop" for yourself. Take a break, let go of the need for control, and trust that the universe has a plan for you. It might be the most powerful thing you ever do.

Here are some tips for you to try as you create your "just stop" process.

1. Prioritize self-care: Make sure to take care of yourself physically, mentally, and emotionally. This could mean taking breaks throughout the day, practicing mindfulness, or setting aside time for a hobby or activity you enjoy.
2. Let go of control: Recognize that you can't control everything and that sometimes, the best thing you can do is to let go and trust the process.
3. Embrace the unknown: Instead of fearing the unknown, embrace it. Remember that some of the best things in life happen when we step out of our comfort zones and try something new.
4. Focus on what truly matters: Identify the things that truly matter to you and prioritize them in your life. This could mean spending more time with loved ones, pursuing a passion project, or focusing on your health.
5. Say no when needed: Learn to say no to things that aren't aligned with your goals or that don't bring you joy. This can be difficult at first, but it's an important part of creating space for the things that truly matter.
6. Trust your intuition: Listen to your intuition and follow your gut. Sometimes, our inner voice knows what's best for us, even if our logical mind doesn't quite understand it yet.
7. Practice gratitude: Cultivate a sense of gratitude for the things you have in your life. Focusing on what you're grateful for can help you stay positive and focused on what truly matters.
8. Embrace rest: Give yourself permission to rest and recharge. Remember that rest is an important part of the creative process, and it can help you come back to your work feeling refreshed and energized.

9. Collaborate with others: Work with others who share your values and goals. Collaboration can help you achieve more than you could on your own, and it can be a great way to tap into new ideas and perspectives.

10. Keep learning: Stay curious and continue to learn new things. This can help you stay engaged and inspired in your work and your life, and it can help you continue to grow and evolve as a person.

Genesis 21:17

"And God heard the voice of the lad; and the angel of God called to Hagar out of heaven, and said unto her, What aileth thee, Hagar? fear not; for God hath heard the voice of the lad where he is."

CHAPTER 14
God Has Heard Your Prayer
EMERGENCY DEPARTMENT PSYCHIATRIC
FORENSICS SOCIAL WORKER
CANISE LEWIS

AT THE AGE OF 32, I found myself divorced and raising a three-year-old little boy as a single mother, whom my ex-husband and I had adopted on the day of his birth. It was especially painful for me because we had committed to raising this child in a two-parent home; promising the biological mother that me and my ex intended to raise him as she had requested in her adoption application. It was for that reason she relinquished her parental rights for us to adopt. I was devastated to have failed in my commitment to parenting this chosen child in an environment I believed to be the best-case scenario. I needed to hear from God. I felt I had failed Him; this child; the agency that supported this adoption (DCFS); friends and family. I was ashamed of myself; and unreasonably fearful of everything and everyone.

I woke up out of my sleep, early one morning, before sunrise; remembering a bible story I read years ago during family worship. The story of Abraham, Sarai, and Hagar. Great story.

The story begins with Abraham and Sarai being of old age; way beyond their child-bearing years. Their desire to become parents was a yearning for both Abraham and Sarai. God had promised them a child; however, due to their age; Sarai suggested that Abraham take on a handmaid, and impregnate her; which would allow Sarai to have children. Abraham did not argue. He went in unto Hagar and she conceived. When Sarai saw that Hagar conceived, the bible states, "her mistress was despised in her eyes." Interesting observation: Sarai had referred to Hagar before her pregnancy as a handmaid. After she conceived, she referred to her as a mistress. Nonetheless, this story goes on to record the contentious relationship that developed between Abram, Sarah, and Hagar, leading up to, and after Sarah gave birth to Isaac, her first child with Abraham. Sarah begins to notice Ishmael's disrespect for Abraham's way of worship and becomes angry. She told Abraham he had to get rid of Hagar and Ishmael. After all, Sarah had despised Hagar since her pregnancy with Ishmael. Abraham was not happy with Sarah's request; it pained him tremendously to kick out his flesh and blood. Interestingly enough, God told Abraham to listen to Sarah, his wife. Abraham packed food and water (a semblance of child support) and told Hagar she and the boy had to leave. Hagar and Ishmael wandered in the wilderness; eventually running out of food and water. Hagar was emotionally traumatized watching her son hungry, thirsty, angry, and near death. At nighttime, Hagar walked away from Ishmael; lifted her voice, and wept mightily. As she cried out, soliciting help from God; an angel of God called out to Hagar saying; "What aileth thee?" Or why are you crying? *Fear not; for God has heard the prayer of the lad where he is."* Now remember, Ishmael was not in a good place, physically and emotionally. His father just kicked him and his mother out of the home he had provided for them for many years. Ishmael was full of rage, hate, and disrespect for God's ways, and near death due to hunger and thirst.

As a single mother with a male child who was emotionally angry, and in rage his father left him and his mother. I put myself in Hagar's shoes, agonizing with God as well. But when I read what the angel of God told her… "God heard the prayer of the lad where he is" I begin to cry myself. God heard the prayer of the lad where he is. I was comforted beyond belief to know that God also has heard the prayer of my son; and also promised to provide for him like he did for Ishmael. As a single mother, the best emotion of all time is whenever someone is kind and nice to your child or children. To have the God of heaven send an angel to tell me He has heard my child's prayer; was far better to me than God answering my prayer.

Many years have passed since my son was a child, and there were many a day that I cried out to God to hear the prayers of my son. God opened my eyes to see how he blessed my son; just like He opened the eyes of Hagar; providing her with plenty of water, housing, and a future for her son. My son has since graduated college, purchased a home, and is dating a wonderful young lady. God is good to all.

Matthew 21:22

"And all things, whatsoever ye shall ask in prayer, believing, ye shall receive."

CHAPTER 15
My (God's) House

ATTORNEY
CHARMAINE SINGLETON

FROM JANUARY 2019 until June 2022, I was periodically looking for a house to live in but could not find the right one. Then in July 2022, I was talking to a sister-friend Mary concerning my house-hunting journey. Mary quietly listened to me and then asked if I ever wrote down in specific detail the type of house I wanted. I replied no I had not. Mary then told me to write down my heart's desire as if I were speaking to God and then conclude with the words "exceedingly and abundantly" and watch God show up and show out. I did what Mary advised me to do, I wrote down I wanted a house, that would be a "sanctuary" that was on the corner of the block. I wanted the house to have at least 4 bedrooms (that could comfortably fit all the items I had in storage and the items that were in my then apartment), an office, a den, and a beautiful comforting backyard. A place where I could hide away, but still be able to entertain family and friends. That God would bless me with the resources to pay for the house and that I would not lack anything. I concluded with the words "exceedingly and abundantly".

A week later on a Friday night at about 11 pm, I was on the computer and found a house that appeared to satisfy all my needs. I immediately emailed my realtor, Erica, and wrote; I think I found my house and provided her the address. Two minutes later I emailed Erica again and wrote, I know I found my house. On Saturday, as I was entering a church for a women's event, Erica called me and asked if I wanted to see the house (that I emailed her about), I stated yes, and she stated it may take a couple of days to set up an appointment and I stated okay. I forgot about the house and turned my attention to the women's event which concerned God's provision and blessing you in unexpected places. As I was leaving the church building, I received a text from Erica stating that I could view the house on the very next day, Sunday, because the owner was having an open house. I replied to Erica's text and stated that we could meet at the house on Sunday afternoon.

Erica and I met at the house, prayed first for a transfer of wealth, and then entered the residence. The owner's friend, Charles, who was showing the house, appeared to give me his full attention, even though others were also in attendance. He told us about the house in specific detail, which matched every detail that I had written down and more. Even though my bank account did not suggest that I was going to be able to afford the house, I knew that the house was mine. I put in an offer on the house and waited. The owner asked to meet with me, which I obliged. She gave me and Erica a personal tour of the house pointing out every detail. Two hours later she was convinced that I was the right person to take care of what was once her "dream house". Within less than 60 days, God heard my prayer and brought heaven to earth and answered my prayer exceedingly and abundantly more than I could ask for or even think, as well as Erica's prayer and allowed me to purchase my new home. In turn, I promised God that every chance that was afforded unto me, I would speak of His goodness, knowing that my sanctuary (house) is His. And every morning when I can look into my backyard I am reminded how God moved heaven and earth to bless me. Speak it and it shall be so, in God's perfect timing.

Isaiah 41:10

"Fear thou not; for I am with thee: be not dismayed; for I am thy God: I will strengthen thee; yea, I will help thee; yea, I will uphold thee with the right hand of my righteousness."

CHAPTER 16
Determined Beyond Measure

OWNER AND FITNESS EXPERT AT SHETRAINS
FITNESS

SHAYLA ST CLAIR

IN LATE FEBRUARY OF 2020, my dream of becoming a full-time Fitness Trainer would soon become a reality. At that point in my life, I was beginning to spiral. Balancing the demands of work, graduate school, and home responsibilities had taken a toll on both my mental and physical well-being. The weight of it all had become too much.

It was clear that a change was needed, and that change was my job. When my job security came into question, it was a sign for me to make a bold move. It was as if a light switched on in my mind. That's when the world of entrepreneurship entered my horizon, and I drafted a 90-day plan to exit my current situation.

Was I scared? Absolutely.

Was I uncertain? Absolutely.

Was I determined? Beyond measure.

Researching local gyms led me to a friend who was success-fully training clients online through a fitness app. Even though he lacked formal fitness training, his business was still thriving. Given our friendship, I was intrigued to learn more. He then introduced me to my mentor, Brandon Carter, known as "King Keto," the visionary behind High Ticket Trainer.

While still pursuing a graduate degree in fitness, I was presented with an opportunity to join High Ticket Trainer. It was a hard decision, but I had to make a choice. On March 8, 2020, I joined High Ticket Trainer and my journey towards my purpose began.

Within a month, I was matching my previous salary. It was an empowering feeling that resonated deep within me. Coaching a group of six women in my program, and witnessing their transfor-mations in weight, mood, and better quality of life, solidified my path.

By the end of April, I had doubled my salary. When May arrived, I made the audacious decision to quit my job—60 days into my 90-day plan. Taking a two-week vacation, I never looked back. The investment of $7,000 in High Ticket Trainer had paid off, and I celebrated earning my first $10,000.

Fast forward to today, I am now collaborating with and nurturing the dreams and aspirations of countless women. As a coach for Brandon Carter, I'm assisting numerous personal trainers in establishing their online fitness businesses. Recently, I launched my digital marketing agency, aimed at helping personal trainers and local gyms expand through organic cold and warm outreach, sales, and retention.

This remarkable journey wouldn't have been possible without a foundation of belief. For years, I harbored the desire for such success, but it was the unexpected challenges at work that ignited my faith in myself. I learned to ask for what I wanted, and as I did, opportunities began to unfold before me.

Luke 1:37

"For with God nothing shall be impossible."

CHAPTER 17

My Journey Has Just Begun

STUDENT, CLARK ATLANTA UNIVERSITY
MERRY ADELEYE

FROM AN EARLY AGE, I always knew I wanted to go to a college away from home. Not necessarily because I wanted to be away from my family, but because I knew that there was so much more to view and experience outside of Sacramento. The only flipside to that was the fact that my mom didn't want me to go away. She told me that I could attend any school in the state of California, but that still didn't sound very appealing to me. When I was at school one day during my junior year, my friends and I were on the topic of college. I remember one of them telling me that she wanted to attend Spelman, before this I don't think I had ever heard of it. Being from California, going to an HBCU wasn't heavily pushed, at least for me and the students around me. This was around the time that I started looking into more historically black colleges and thought that going to a school with others like me sounded better than what I would experience at a predominantly white institution. I did some research into Spelman and talked to a friend of mine who goes there. She told me a lot about the adjustments and culture shock that she experienced going to Atlanta from Sacramento. She gave me insight about the AUC (Atlanta University Center) which consists of Clark, Morehouse, Spelman, and Morris Brown which recently got their accreditation back. The way that she described the AUC and explained how there is no place like it with the endless connections and opportunities as well as being surrounded by what felt like family made me fall in love with it immediately. When I found out about Clark Atlanta, I instantly stuck with it. I felt like this school had so much to offer no matter what field you decided to go into and produced greatness. I brought the idea of going to school in Atlanta to my mother and of course, she wasn't on board. She didn't want me on the complete opposite of the country without family to call in case of an emergency which is completely understandable. I never thought I'd see the day that we moved to the South. When my Dad told me that he had a job opportunity in Atlanta, I honestly couldn't believe it. Moving from the only place I knew as home and coming to Georgia felt so surreal, it still does. Though I was sad to leave behind my friends and family, I knew that there would be ample opportunities to make this move. We moved at the start of the second semester of my junior year, so I was able to experience Mock Trial, FBLA, Chic Fil A Leadership, and many other clubs and opportunities that I otherwise would not have experienced at my school in California. Deciding to come to Clark after moving to Atlanta was a no-brainer. So far, I can honestly say that I am completely happy and satisfied with my commitment to CAU. I have only completed my first semester and have already begun to create a name for myself and network throughout the AUC. I have learned many life skills from my Sociology and Composition professors who teach from the standpoint of a family member who wants what is best rather than a teacher who is only worried about money. I was offered an internship at the DA's office by a CAU alumna, and have met people who share common interests with me. I am excited to see what God has in store for me at Clark Atlanta and most importantly, this journey has shown me that if it is meant to happen, it will come to fruition.

Paulo Coelho

"And, when you want something, all the universe
conspires in helping you to achieve it."

THE UNIVERSE ALWAYS PROVIDES

In this compilation book of extraordinary stories, we have journeyed through the remarkable lives of individuals who harnessed the power of determination and belief to manifest their deepest desires. These tales are a testament to the boundless human spirit and the incredible capacity we possess to shape our destinies. From dreams that defied the odds to ambitions that soared to new heights, these stories are a beacon of hope, reminding us that with unwavering faith and relentless perseverance, the possibilities are endless. As we conclude this collection, let these stories be an enduring source of inspiration, encouraging us all to embrace our dreams and turn them into reality. In the stories of these remarkable yet ordinary individuals, we find the universal truth that our desires are not merely wishes; they are the blueprints of our futures.

I invite you to take a moment to reflect on your own journey. Life is a collection of stories, and yours is just as important as the ones you've just read about.

Turn the page and find a blank canvas waiting for your words. Share your personal achievements, your dreams, or the moments that changed your life. Because, in this space, your story becomes a part of this tapestry of inspiration.

Believe in your story, for it has the power to inspire others!

With gratitude,
Janice

Notes

Notes

Notes

130

Notes